Growing in the Christian Life

HARVEST HOUSE PUBLISHERS
EUGENE, OREGON

Cover by Koechel Peterson & Associates, Inc., Minneapolis, Minnesota

Cover photo © Hemera / Thinkstock

GROWING IN THE CHRISTIAN LIFE
Stonecroft Bible Studies
Copyright © 2013 by Stonecroft Ministries, Inc.
Published by Harvest House Publishers
Eugene, Oregon 97408
www.harvesthousepublishers.com

ISBN 978-0-7369-5569-0 (pbk.)
ISBN 978-0-7369-5570-6 (eBook)

Printed in the United States of America

19 20 21 / VP-CD / 10

Contents

Acknowledgments

Stonecroft wishes to acknowledge and thank Janice Mayo Mathers for her dedication in serving the Lord through Stonecroft. Speaker, author, and member of the Board of Directors, Jan is the primary author of the revised Stonecroft Bible Studies. We appreciate her love for God's Word and her love for people who need Him. Special thanks goes to the team who prayed for Jan, and those who edited, designed, and offered their creative input to make these studies accessible to all. Stonecroft is also grateful to Lucille Sollenberger, who is now with the Lord she loved and served, for the original development of this study.

Welcome to Stonecroft Bible Studies!

I t doesn't matter where you've been or what you've done...God wants to be in relationship with you. And one place He tells you about Himself is in His Word—the Bible. Whether the Bible is familiar or new to you, its contents will transform your life and bring answers to your biggest questions.

Gather with people in your communities—women, men, couples, young and old alike—and find out together how the Bible's book of James is like a handbook for life. You'll see how James connects faith with behavior—behavior based on God's principles that will improve your relationships and the quality of your life.

Each chapter of *Growing in the Christian Life* includes discussion questions to stir up meaningful conversation, specific Scripture verses to investigate, and time for prayer to connect with God and each other.

Discover more of God and His ways through this small-group exploration of the Bible.

Tips for Using This Study

This book has several features that make it easy to use and helpful for your life:

- The page number or numbers given after every Bible reference are keyed to the page numbers in the *Abundant Life Bible*. This paperback Bible uses the New Living Translation, a translation in straightforward, up-to-date language. We encourage you to obtain a copy through your group leader or at stonecroft.org.

- Each chapter ends with a section called "Thoughts, Notes, and Prayer Requests." Use this space for notes or for thoughts that come to you during your group time or study, as well as prayer requests.

- In the back of the book you will find "Journal Pages"—a space available for writing down how the study is changing your life or any other personal thoughts, reactions, and reflections.

- Please make this book and study your own. We encourage you to use it and mark it in any way that helps you grow in your relationship with God!

If you find this study helpful, you may want to investigate other resources from Stonecroft. Please take a look at "Stonecroft Resources" in the back of the book or online at stonecroft.org/store.

---

stonecroft.org

1

Christian Faith
James 1:1-4

I rang the doorbell of my friend's home, dreading what I would find. On my last visit several weeks before she had been emaciated, her skin gray and her eyes lifeless and sunken. The terrible and fatal disease of scleroderma was gradually capturing her body, turning it into cement, immobilizing her with excruciating pain.

To my surprise, her cheerful voice called out for me to come in. I found her sitting up in bed, her eyes sparkling with a smile that lit up her face. "Marcia!" I cried in delight. "What has happened to you?"

She smiled. "I started thanking God."

She explained that she'd been reading her Bible one day and came across 1 Thessalonians 5:18 (page 907), which says to be thankful in all circumstances. "I told God that I wouldn't lie to Him," she said. "I told Him I could never be thankful for this pain or for the fact that I won't live to see my sons be married. But I told Him I would start being thankful for other, legitimate things."

She told me that every day since then she had begun her morning by being thankful. "I thanked Him for my house, for the birds singing outside my window, and for the beautiful blue sky—my list grew longer each day and I couldn't believe what started to happen. My attitude of thankfulness took me into a deeper level of intimacy with

God than I'd ever before experienced. In fact, it's been so wonderful that one day I actually heard myself say, 'God, thank you for this disease that has brought me so much closer to you!'"

I looked at the glow on Marcia's face and could only marvel at the wonderful power of God to relieve even the most hopeless circumstances.

Now it has been almost 12 years since that visit. Against all odds, Marcia has lived to see both of her sons married and has three grandchildren who she delights in. Inexplicably, the relentless march of scleroderma through her body has stopped, allowing her to engage more fully in life. No one knows how long the remission will last. In the meantime Marcia says, "I'm just so thankful for all God has brought into my life as a result of my disease."

You are going to love the book of James! I am excited for us to do this study together because it overflows with principles that will change your life when you put them into practice.

Prayer

God, let faith continue strong in me—I know that you have not given me a spirit of fear and timidity, but of power, love, and self-discipline. Let me hold on to the pattern of wholesome teaching that is shaped by the faith and love that I have in Christ Jesus. Help me, through the power of the Holy Spirit who lives within me, to carefully guard the precious truth that has been entrusted to me (2 Timothy 1:5b,7,13-14, page 914).

The Author

More than one man named James is referred to in the New Testament. In fact, two of Jesus' disciples shared the name. However, the author of the book of James was not one of the 12 disciples—he was Jesus' half brother.

Knowing this connection gives insight into the heart of this godly man. When we consider that James and Jesus grew up together in the same family, doing things such as chores, playing with each other, and teasing their sisters, it is remarkable that James was able to make the transition from seeing Jesus as his sibling to seeing Him as his Savior! It would have required an extraordinary level of God-given faith. No wonder the theme woven into this wonderful book is faith. James lived what he wrote about.

The transition did not happen automatically, however. What do the following verses say about Jesus' family's reaction to His ministry and purpose?

John 7:1-5 (page 815)

Mark 3:20-21 (page 763)

It is not clear when James became convinced his brother was truly the Son of God. Perhaps it was after Jesus' resurrection. Read 1 Corinthian 15:4-7 (page 879).

The resurrection of Jesus was huge news. Although He had told His followers this would happen, no one could quite grasp the reality until they saw Him alive and well after He'd been put to death. Many people had already reported seeing Jesus alive when He appeared to James. It would have been difficult to doubt the word of people you knew and respected, but even more difficult to believe such reports—until you saw for yourself. Once Jesus appeared to James, we see nothing but James' full and unreserved devotion to Jesus as the Son of God. The rest of James' life was spent spreading the gospel.

After Jesus' resurrection and ascension into heaven (Mark 16:19, page 778), James rose in responsibility to become the head of the church in Jerusalem. It was a difficult time for the Christians, who were experiencing both economic and religious oppression. Some remained in Jerusalem while others scattered. It was to these Jewish Christians that James was writing this book, wanting to encourage them and strengthen their faith through the very difficult times in which they were living. James experienced the ultimate testing of his faith around AD 62, when he was martyred, according to Josephus, a first-century historian.

Although James did indeed *pen* the words we are going to read in this letter, the Bible tells us who the true author of this book is in 2 Timothy 3:16-17 (page 915).

Who is the ultimate author of the Bible?

What is the purpose of the Bible?

Christians Who Are Suffering

As we begin our study, you will notice the ancient custom of putting one's name at the beginning of the letter instead of at the end, as we do with the letters we write today. Read James 1:1 (page 930).

How does James refer to himself?

What do you think he meant when he referred to himself as a slave?

James was stating his total commitment to God, indicating that he had placed himself completely under God's authority.

To whom did James address his letter?

Most of the people who first believed that Jesus was the Son of God were Jewish. They established the first Christian churches and, in fact, wrote most of the New Testament. These are the people James is addressing in his book—Jews who believed that Jesus was the Son of God and their long-awaited Messiah. After Jesus' death and resurrection, these Christians were scattered throughout Judea and Samaria due to severe persecution because of their belief in Jesus as the Messiah. Read Acts 8:1 (page 836). At the time James wrote his letter, Jewish Christians were living throughout the known world.

James knew that these Christians were being tested. He wrote to teach them how they could experience joy even in the midst of trials.

Immediately after his greeting, he told his readers what his letter was to address. Read James 1:2-3 (page 930).

To consider trouble or testing as an opportunity for great joy is unnatural by any earthly standard. But this is why this book is so powerful: It will teach us how to process the challenges that enter our lives in a way that will help us, rather than harm us. It will show us how we can experience an attitude of joy in spite of what we are facing.

Faith in the Midst of Difficulty

The secret to the power of this book lies in a little five-letter word tucked into verse three, which is also the book's theme.

What is this word?

Faith is essential to a relationship with Jesus. It is essential to our quality of life! James experienced this truth personally, and he wanted to pass it on to all believers.

How is faith defined in Hebrews 11:1 (page 926)?

Faith gives us both confidence and assurance to walk through each day regardless of what it might hold for us. It is that combination of confidence and assurance that makes endurance possible—and not just endurance but a joy-filled endurance, because it keeps our focus on God and not on our circumstances.

It is also important to note that in this same chapter of Hebrews, verse 6 tells us that *"it is impossible to please God without faith."* God *values* our faith, and that same verse says He rewards our faith! It is impossible to overstate the importance of faith to our lives.

Look at James 1:3 (page 930) again. What will happen when our faith is tested?

Now read verse 4. What is the result of letting our endurance grow?

One of the exquisite benefits of following Jesus is that nothing is wasted. He has the ability to bring purpose and meaning to even the most agonizing experiences if we will trust Him with those times. Imagine a bad thing happening to you, and then imagine needing *nothing* because your faith has made you perfect and complete. Only God could work out something like that.

But let's not spend time imagining. We all experience some painful realities.

Is there a circumstance in your life right now that troubles you? Please share.

Now write a summary of James 1:2-4, incorporating your circumstance into it.

Now tell God that even though you don't completely understand the concept of experiencing joy, you are willing to trust that He can show you what He means in these verses. During this next week, every time you feel anxious or irritated by your circumstance, remind yourself of the words you just wrote down. Let them become a prayer.

Finding Joy in Our Circumstances

The Bible tells us that God controls the course of the world and our destinies (Daniel 2:21, page 668, and 5:23, page 672). It also tells us that God loves us.

According to 1 John 4:9-10 (page 943) how did God show His love to us?

If God is sovereign and if He loves us that much, doesn't it make sense that He will use the circumstances that enter our lives to strengthen us rather than defeat us?

When we acknowledge God's love for people, including you and me, then the next question that often comes up is why, if God loves us, does He allow bad things to happen? He doesn't always tell us the exact reason why difficult circumstances happen. But He does tell us that whatever comes into our lives is allowed by the same love that sent Jesus to the cross (Romans 8:32, page 863). God loves us enough to allow us to suffer for His glory and our good (Romans 8:28, page 863). And God gives us the great privilege of sharing in Christ's sufferings (Philippians 3:10, page 901).

In her books, Joni Eareckson Tada has documented her personal struggle to find joy in her circumstances. When she was 17, she dove into a river and was seriously injured, becoming a quadriplegic. Some 40 years later she writes,

> My affliction has stretched my hope, made me know Christ better, helped me long for truth, led me to repentance of sin, goaded me to give thanks in times of sorrow, increased my faith and strengthened my character. Being in this wheelchair has meant knowing *Him* better, feeling His pleasure every day.

She quotes Henry Frost, who said, "I feel it would have been nothing short of a calamity to have missed the physical suffering through which I have passed."[1]

Joni is a vivid, indisputable example of someone who, by God's grace, has chosen to consider her circumstances as a reason for joy. By doing so, she has become greater than her tragedy. She has become a victor rather than a victim.

Have you ever asked, "Why is this happening to me?" It's a common question to ask when life veers off of the course we thought we were on. In times of heartache or tragedy it's not our natural

inclination to think, *I consider this as an opportunity for joy!* Read
Romans 5:3-4 (page 860).

What words are mentioned in both this Romans passage and
James 1:2-4?

The concept of rejoicing right in the middle of problems and
troubles is the common theme. God uses this joyful attitude to help
develop our character and our hope.
Read Hebrews 10:35-36 (page 926).

What will bring you a great reward according to these verses?

Our faith in God increases our ability to endure, which builds our
confidence, which results in experiencing all that He has promised us.
We can view trials as catalysts that focus our attention, and sometimes the attention of others, on God.

What does Jesus say in Matthew 5:11-12 (page 736)?

Jesus wants us to know how to avoid destructive, debilitating pain and sorrow by choosing to be joyful in the midst of trials and persecution. He develops joy within us in and through trials, so that our faith will grow strong and our endurance will increase.

A Temporary Situation

What does 1 Peter 1:6-7 (page 934) say about the duration of these trials?

These trials are temporary. Even though we have to endure them now on earth, they will result in our growth and in God's honor when we are joyful through the experience. He knows that to choose joy in the midst of suffering is counter to our human nature. Yet He supplies us with the ability to choose joy, to be truly glad because of the hope that is before us. In the process, we discover that our trials cause our enduring faith to become genuinely clear. Our enduring faith reflects Christ, and that is good for everyone!

It's easy to feel that God is punishing us when things go differently than we planned. But while some pain is the result of our own poor decisions, other pain is the result of life in general. In the Old Testament book of Job we read about a good man who suffered deeply. In the depth of his pain he noted, *"How short is life, how full of trouble"* (Job 14:1, page 397). But Job kept his eyes on God, and in the end God restored him.

In what ways have you tried to diagnose the reason or purpose of your past sufferings?

What does Proverbs 3:5 (page 482) say?

God sees the whole picture—past, present, and future. We can trust Him because He knows what is going to happen today, tomorrow, and beyond and how to help us. We don't have access to that information. We have access to only the present moment, which makes our understanding extremely undependable compared to that of an all-knowing God.

The more we trust God, the more spiritual maturity we gain and the more natural it becomes to respond to our circumstances in a healthy way. Read Colossians 2:6-7 (page 903).

What must we do after we have received Jesus as our Lord?

What will the result be once we follow Christ and build our lives upon Him?

As our roots grow down deep into Jesus, our faith will grow strong, and we will become more thankful and spiritually mature. Read the following passages and note what we can do to make our roots grow strong.

1 Peter 2:1-3 (page 935)

Psalm 1:1-3 (page 415)

2 Timothy 3:16-17 (page 915)

Regular Bible reading is essential to our spiritual growth and health. God's Word keeps our thinking on the right track. It protects us from erroneous conclusions and unhealthy attitudes. As we study God's Word, the Holy Spirit fills us with wisdom, faith, and joy!

A Changed Attitude

God's Word not only fills us with joy, but it also calls us to find joy in the middle of troubles in our lives.

What is God's will for our lives, according to 1 Thessalonians 5:16-18 (page 907)?

The message is clear. God wants to help us cultivate an attitude of thankfulness and joy. I know that, depending on what you have experienced in your past or are experiencing now, this may seem impossible. Please keep your mind open to what God wants to show you in this study. Will you be willing to experiment with what we've read? Copy your personalized version of James 1:2-3 onto a 3-by-5 card or input it into your smartphone and keep it with you. Every time your circumstance comes to mind, read or listen to the verses.

> God is always expressing His love for us—even in situations we cannot understand.

The purpose of this study is to help us grow by applying the truths we learn in God's Word. It will be beneficial to read the book of James as many times as possible during this study. It has only five chapters, so it doesn't take long to read. As you read you will find new insight and greater understanding.

Before you sit down to read,

- ask God to help you understand what you read.
- ask God to keep your mind focused on what you're reading.
- ask God to let you hear what He says to you.
- ask God to make you willing to do what He asks.

————————— *Personal Reflection and Application* —————————

From this chapter,

I see...

I believe...

I will...

❦

Prayer

Lord, I understand that my trials will show that my faith is genuine. I understand that my faith is being tested as fire tests and purifies gold—though my faith is far more precious than gold. So help my faith remain strong through trials, so that I will bring you much praise and glory and honor. I love you even though I have never seen you. And though I do not see you now, still I trust you; and I rejoice with a glorious, inexpressible joy. I know the reward for trusting you will be the salvation of my soul (1 Peter 1:7-9, page 934).

Thoughts, Notes, and Prayer Requests

2

Christian Faith Is Tested
James 1:5-18

Michael Blumenthal, former US secretary of the treasury, grew up in Nazi Germany. He saw his father barely escape with his life from a concentration camp, after which his family emigrated to wartime Shanghai. He watched how differently people reacted to being stripped of all their possessions and thrust into a foreign environment. It wasn't just physical possessions they lost, but their identity as well. The immigrants spoke only German, which was a useless language in Shanghai. Being a successful lawyer in Germany was worthless in Shanghai. Being a famous German journalist meant nothing to the Chinese, who had never heard of such a person.

Blumenthal's experience in Shanghai became his measuring stick for evaluating people throughout his career. While talking with them he'd silently ask himself, *How would you do in Shanghai?* He comments,

> I have always thought, after observing how people reacted in this environment…that what counts in life is not who you are or where you come from but the inner resources that you bring to bear…The trick is not how well you deal with success, but how well you deal with adversity.[2]

This is exactly what James is doing in his letter—he is teaching Christians how to flourish amid adversity.

Prayer

Lord, I know that when I go through deep waters, you will be with me. When I go through rivers of difficulty, I will not drown. When I walk through the fire of oppression, I will not be burned up; the flames will not consume me. For you are the Lord, my God...my Savior (Isaiah 43:2-3a, page 550).

To begin, let's review some key points from the first chapter.

According to James 1:2 (page 930), how does God want us to react to our challenging circumstances?

According to James 1:3, what will God do when we face trouble?

According to James 1:4, what is the result?

God's Offer of Wisdom

Today's lesson is full of practical wisdom that you will find to be both helpful and encouraging. The verse we begin with is one of the most encouraging. Do you ever long for help in making a decision or in deciding what the best course of action might be? God understands and makes a wonderful offer to us. Read James 1:5 (page 930).

What is the result of our asking for wisdom?

Think about the full implication of this verse. Our wisdom is limited to our past and current experience. We don't know what the future holds, but God does. Nothing is hidden from Him. Even more, this verse tells us that He has made His wisdom available to us. All we have to do is ask!

How would you describe God, according to verse 5?

He will not be stingy with His wisdom. He will be generous. He will even be patient with our asking. He *wants* us to ask for wisdom, because He wants us to be well-equipped in all circumstances!

According to the Merriam-Webster dictionary, wisdom is described as knowledge, insight, good sense, and judgment.

God's Definition of Wisdom

The Bible takes the definition of wisdom even further.

According to James 3:17 (page 931), what are the seven attributes of the wisdom that comes from God?

Which, if any, of these attributes surprise you?

What is the common theme among them?

There is nothing self-centered about godly wisdom. Wisdom is seeing things from God's point of view.

In which circumstance in your life do you need God's wisdom right now?

Tune your ears to wisdom,
and concentrate on understanding.

—Proverbs 2:2 (page 482)

What do the following verses say about wisdom?

Job 28:28 (page 405)

Proverbs 3:7 (page 482)

Psalm 111:10 (page 466)

Proverbs 1:7 (page 481)

What is the common thread in these verses?

What is an appropriate response you can make to these verses regarding the circumstance in which you need God's wisdom?

To fear God means to hold Him in reverence and awe. When we do that, it changes our behavior. We want to turn *toward* God and away from evil. Our faith in God has both the elements of belief and action. The combination of having faith in God and acting in accordance with our faith is one of the main points of the book of James.

> "Wisdom comes privately from God as a by-product of right decisions, godly reactions, and the application of spiritual principles to daily circumstances."
>
> —*Charles Swindoll*

Living with a Divided Mind

Read James 1:6-8 (page 930).

What or who do you have a tendency to put your faith in besides God?

There are so many things that can add to or detract from our faith. We say our faith is only in God, but unfortunately we often fail to live like our faith is solely in Him. Sometimes our degree of faith is affected by our own self-confidence or lack thereof. It can be influenced by our own abilities or our family's abilities, by the balance in our bank account, or by our time constraints. In reality, many different circumstances may have an impact on the level of faith we have in God.

How do verses 6 and 8 describe a person whose faith is divided?

Think of a time when you were unsettled in regard to something you were trusting God for. How did you handle the unsettledness?

I can remember some times when I was unsettled with God's timing, and I decided to take matters into my own hands. Of course, it never turned out well. It's crazy to think that my idea might be better than His plan, but it happens! I forget to act out my faith.

What does verse 7 say the result of such thinking will be?

It is sobering. Think back on your own life. Has there been a time when God might not have answered your prayer because you weren't placing your faith in Him? Please share.

It should be easy for us to have faith in God because He is all-knowing, all-powerful, and all-loving. After all, we tend to have faith in material things even though they are faulty and break down over time. When you step into an elevator, do you feel the need to tug on the cables to help you reach the floor you want to go to? We also have faith in people even though they are fallible and not always trustworthy. When boarding a plane, do you slip the pilot a note suggesting the best way to get you to your destination?

Things and people can fail us, but we trust them without a second thought. But when it comes to the Creator of the universe, we often feel compelled to lend Him our expertise! No wonder God finds us unstable.

The eleventh chapter of Hebrews (pages 926-927) is sometimes called the "Hall of Faith" because it gives a list of people who lived during the Old Testament period who put their faith in God. We read about Sarah, who gave birth to a son at the age of 90, and the Israelites, who watched the walls of Jericho crumble after marching repeatedly around the perimeter. We also read about Noah, who built an ark to save his family from the Flood. In each example given in this chapter, the people both believed and obeyed. It was both a mental and a physical exercise they undertook—and in the process, they saw God work again and again and again.

What does Ephesians 4:14 (page 897) call those who are carried about by the wind of new beliefs?

You cannot trust and doubt at the same time, just as you cannot face two directions at once. That's what causes instability. A double-minded person is restless and insecure, seeking advice from one person after another. Their advice differs, of course, and the indecision of the double-minded person grows. God wants us to come to Him. Complete dependence on Him will calm the ocean waves of doubt and indecision. It will smooth out into confidence and clear direction.

The Problem of Wealth

The next three verses have to do with material wealth and its potential to interfere with our faith. Read James 1:9-11 (page 930).

What message do you hear from this passage?

When people become followers of Jesus, it has a leveling effect. God views us the same. Our level of material wealth has no bearing on our relationship with Jesus. A relationship with Him gives new worth to a person in poor circumstances and puts the riches of a wealthy person in proper perspective. It is no longer about our material well-being; instead, it is about our spiritual well-being—our position in Christ. Regardless of our financial status, *we have equal access to God's riches!*

We all have our own definition of what we consider material wealth. How would you define spiritual wealth?

Everyone should crave spiritual wealth. We should do everything possible to increase it! Spiritual wealth will never let us down. But what does this passage say will happen to our material wealth?

As we put our trust in God and follow Him, He will endow us with a spiritual wealth that will enable us to rise above any circumstance this life hands us. It will fill us with confidence, peace, and well-being no matter what storms sweep through our lives.

A Perspective That Looks Forward

According to James 1:12, who does God bless?

It is easy to forget that this life we are in right now is only a moment in the whole spectrum of time. Although God gives us blessings now, eternity is where the full rewards wait.

James reminds the people he was writing to that although they were experiencing severe persecution, God would bless them for their endurance now and reward them in eternity.

What are some ways Christians experience persecution today?

Have you personally experienced persecution? How did you respond?

The apostles experienced extreme persecution for their faith. Read Acts 5:40-42 (page 834) and note how they responded to persecution.

It circles right back to the beginning of James' letter — to maintain an attitude of joy regardless of our circumstances. Why did the apostles rejoice?

After the apostles were beaten they were warned never to speak about Jesus again. According to verse 42, how did they react to the warning?

Can you picture that? They went daily to the Temple, which was a very public building, in order to tell people about Jesus! Their faith in Jesus filled them with joy, which increased their endurance and built up their confidence, which then amplified their faith and filled them with joy. What an incredible cycle.

Read 1 Peter 4:12-14 (pages 936-937). What will the result of the persecution be?

I know from personal experience that whenever I go through a very difficult time, I am always comforted the most by someone else who has experienced it, felt it, and lived through it. Whatever pain you have experienced in your past, or are feeling now, or will feel in the future, Jesus has partnered and will partner with you through it, walking beside you, infusing you with His strength. As a result, you can experience joy in the midst of your circumstances.

Jesus suffered immeasurable agony for us, and He will be with us when we suffer for Him as well. As the name *Christian* becomes more and more a target for disdain and ridicule, it can be daunting to proclaim it with assurance.

How does Mark 8:38 (page 769) respond to this issue?

Have you ever been in a group of people where you kept your Christian beliefs hidden? What were the circumstances?

Many of us have found ourselves in such a position, but know this: God understands when our courage fails us. Be honest about it with Him and ask Him to infuse you with His courage each time He gives you an opportunity to share your faith. In fact, why don't we take a minute right now and ask God to help us with this?

Struggling with Temptation

Read James 1:13-15 (page 930).

This is a powerful group of verses because it shows us exactly how we end up doing the wrong things.

Where does temptation come from?

Temptation comes not from God, but from within ourselves! Our *thoughts* form our desires. What influences our thoughts?

If someone struggles with excessive spending, the struggle may be fiercest when they are in a store, online, or poring over a catalog. These are places where the desire to spend can be greatly enhanced. Therefore, every time they go into a store or browse through a catalog, they are making the purposeful choice to expose themselves to potential temptation. They might be able to withstand the temptation, but the more they are surrounded by it, the harder it may be to overcome it. As a result, they might yield to the temptation to spend excessively, which could put them into debt. This downward cycle can lead to various troubles and trials and, according to verse 15, lead to sinful actions and eventually death.

Temptation is not sinful. We all experience temptation. Still, *feeding* the temptation by opening ourselves to an area of weakness (for example, running to the store, running to the refrigerator, or running to an online pornography site) puts us in harm's way and ultimately can lead to sin. The seed for sin is sown in the soil of your thoughts. You choose how fertile the soil is by what you allow to feed your thoughts.

We also know that the enemy of our soul wants to kill, steal, and destroy us. He brings temptation to try to derail us. We will read later that James tells us to resist him and he will flee. In Ephesians, Paul instructs us on protecting ourselves against the schemes of the devil:

A final word: Be strong in the Lord and in his mighty power. Put on all of God's armor so that you will be able to stand firm against all strategies of the devil. For we are not fighting against flesh-and-blood enemies, but against evil rulers and authorities of the unseen world, against mighty powers in this dark world, and against evil spirits in the heavenly places.

Therefore, put on every piece of God's armor so you will be able to resist the enemy in the time of evil. Then after the battle you will still be standing firm. Stand your ground, putting on the belt of truth and the body armor of God's righteousness. For shoes, put on the peace that comes from the Good News so that you will be fully prepared. In addition to all of these, hold

*up the shield of faith to stop the fiery arrows of the devil. Put
on salvation as your helmet, and take the sword of the Spirit,
which is the word of God* (Ephesians 6:10-17, page 898).

Sin is birthed in our thoughts, and the struggle can be ongoing.
Read Romans 7:18-20 (page 862).

It comes down to our power of choice. Read Romans 8:5-8 (page
862).

How can we experience *"life and peace"*?

This next verse is an important verse for living your life in a way
that will honor God. Read 1 Corinthians 10:13 (page 876).

What four statements does this verse make about temptation
and God?

Isn't that amazing? Which statement do you find most
encouraging?

Let's take a minute and thank God for His faithfulness that gives us a way to escape every single temptation!

Guarding Our Hearts and Minds

What does the Bible tell us to do with our sinful desires in Colossians 3:5 (page 903)?

How do you think we can actually *put to death* our sinful desires?

It happens in our mind, doesn't it? With God's help we can slam the door on debilitating thoughts and refuse to put ourselves in a position of temptation.

There are five distinct steps leading to sin:

1. A thought enters our mind and rather than reject it outright we mull it over, letting the temptation form.

2. The thought is captured by our imagination—we taste it, feel it, and see it.

3. Our thoughts become tangled in our imagination, and we feel delight in the possibility of experiencing what we're thinking about.

4. Our thoughts become trapped by the imagination, and we begin to rationalize what we want to do.

5. Our thoughts lead us to act on our sinful desire.

Proverbs 4:23 (page 483) helps us. What does it say?

"Above all else"! Our heart is at the center of our lives. What is held in our heart often starts in our mind with our thoughts. Our thoughts determine our words and our behavior. No wonder we are to guard our hearts above all else!

The One We Can Depend On

Read James 1:16-18 (page 930). What comes from God?

Look at the last thought—that out of all creation, we are God's *"prized possession."* As a believer, have you ever stopped to consider that God prizes you? And not only that, but He's not going to change His mind about you, because He will never change! It's so wonderful to know we are *that* loved by Almighty God, the Creator of the universe!

Personal Reflection and Application

From this chapter,

I see…

I believe…

I will…

Prayer

God, I am convinced that nothing can ever separate me from your love. Neither death nor life, neither angels nor demons, neither my fears for today nor my worries about tomorrow—not even the powers of hell can separate me from your love. No power in the sky above or in the earth below—indeed, nothing in all creation will ever be able to separate me from your love that is revealed in Christ Jesus my Lord (Romans 8:38-39, page 863).

─────── *Thoughts, Notes, and Prayer Requests* ───────

3

Christian Faith Is Active
James 1:19-27

I am an addict—I have been for about ten years now. My family has threatened on more than one occasion to stage an intervention. It all started when I decided to lay a small brick patio outside the dining-room door. It was heavy work, hauling the gravel, sand, and bricks, but not hard work. My mind was free to wander pleasantly as I laid the bricks side by side, and I found the work immensely satisfying—plus the finished product was spectacular! *I loved it.* So I decided to enlarge it and add another level for interest. The next summer I laid a small brick patio at the garage door and later enlarged it, extending it the depth of the house. Since then, every summer I've created another small brick patio somewhere around our house. I have laid literally thousands of bricks.

Here is what I've learned about bricklaying. A level foundation is essential! The sand I lay the bricks on can look level to my eye, but if I'm not checking it against a leveling tool, the bricks quickly start to slope. At first it's hardly noticeable, and I can make adjustments. But if I don't re-level the sand, it becomes impossible to lay straight rows. The gaps become larger and larger. The only way to fix it is to pull up the bricks—back to the point where I first started to get off.

It's a lot like our relationship with God. We have to keep lining ourselves up with Him, the level foundation. The moment we rationalize a behavior or attitude, the bubble on our spiritual leveling tool moves slightly off plumb and problems crop up. An unleveled patio is one thing—an unleveled life is quite another. The minute we get even slightly off plumb we need to make an immediate readjustment.

What is our spiritual leveling tool? It is God's Word to us in the Bible as revealed by the Holy Spirit. If we line every thought and action up against the truth of His Word, we will avoid all kinds of heartache.

❦

Prayer

Father, your Word tells me that kind words are like honey—sweet to the soul and healthy for the body, so help me get rid of anger and harsh words. Instead I want to be kind and tenderhearted (Proverbs 16:24, page 492, and Ephesians 4:31-32, page 897).

Speaking and Listening

Today's lesson starts off with a bang—it gets right to the heart of an issue that almost everyone struggles with, and it's an issue that we have all been affected by. Read James 1:19-20 (page 930).

Oh, but it is so much more fun to talk than listen, don't you agree? Especially when what we have to say is so interesting and important! There is incredible power in words, especially negative words. I am amazed at how often a person's sense of self is still being controlled by the negative words someone spoke to them as a child.

Can you think of something someone said to you years ago that still haunts you today?

The Bible has much to say on the subject of speaking and listening, and trust me, the scales are not balanced. God clearly favors our listening or keeping silent over our speaking!

What wisdom do you think there is in this?

Read the following verses and note what they say about speaking.

Proverbs 21:23 (page 496)

Proverbs 18:2 (page 493)

Proverbs 29:20 (page 502)

Proverbs 17:28 (page 493)

Did you notice how often the word *fool* showed up in the same sentence with speaking? It's pretty sobering. Was there a time when you were quick to speak and then later regretted it?

Angry Speech

When you add anger to the mix of your words, real damage can be done. Some people are never able to forget the damaging words someone spoke to them in anger.

> If you knew what you were going to say would have a negative, ongoing impact on someone, would it ever be worth saying it?

The words we speak in anger may come from a self-centered place. We may be reacting to how something has affected, hurt, or frustrated us. There is no room for self-centeredness in the life of a follower of Jesus. Nothing positive comes from such a focus.

Righteous anger is very different than anger birthed from sin. We read in Scripture that righteous anger is a response God expects from His followers when the helpless are being hurt, when worship is misdirected, or when unbelief is present. Unlike the lack of control or outbursts that often accompany sinful anger, righteous anger is under control, under submission to the Lord, and not self-serving. For further study on righteous anger, read Exodus 22:21-24 (page 61) and John 2:13-17 (page 810).

God puts the result of our hastily spoken words in very clear perspective in Matthew 12:36 (page 743). What does it say?

It's difficult to think about, but that is how important our words are. They have tremendous bearing on our spiritual health. As we choose to be slow to speak, slow to become angry, and place our energies into listening, we not only hear the heart of the one who is speaking, but we open ourselves to hearing what God is doing in that moment.

Think about it. How does your speech reflect your relationship with God?

How does anger affect the way people view you as a Christian?

We cannot be too careful because people are always watching, and they're forming their opinions about Jesus based on our behavior. My daughter-in-law put herself through school working as a server in a restaurant. She and her co-workers disliked working the Sunday-after-church crowd because they stayed too long and left stingy tips.

> "Outbursts of anger do not produce the kind of righteous behavior God desires to see in our lives."
> —David P. Nystrom

God's Word: The Antidote to Sin

Read James 1:21 (page 930). What does it tell us to do?

Does the phrase *"filth and evil"* sound a bit overstated in regard to your life? You might be more comfortable using those words to describe someone else. But let's be clear—filth and evil refer to any attitude or behavior that interferes with you and God.

What keeps you from being the person God designed you to be?

What does James 1:21 say God has planted in our hearts?

The Bible is God's communication to us. Within this inspired book are the wisdom, guidance, and instruction we need to become faithful and fruitful followers of Jesus—living lives that bring glory to God and have a positive influence on the world around us.

What does Psalm 119:11 (page 468) say is the correlation between God's Word and our sin?

The more we steep ourselves in God's Word, the less room there will be for evil and filthiness in our hearts. The more familiar we become with His Word, the easier and more natural it is to follow it.

Listening and Doing

It's not enough to just be familiar with God's Word. Read James 1:22-25 (page 930).

Just reading the Bible is not enough. What does it say we are doing if we only listen to God's Word?

Sitting down to read the Bible or playing a Bible CD while we are driving may make us feel good, but it is of little benefit to us if we don't put into practice what it tells us to do. Jesus says the same thing in Luke 11:28 (page 793). Faith is actively believing God's promises.

There is blessing that comes with doing what God tells us to do. Obeying His instructions shows our love for Jesus (John 14:21, page 823) and improves our lives. It's that simple. Consider the example Jesus gave us in the following parable. It is a perfect analogy, which compares someone who listens and then follows God's teaching with someone who only listens. Read Luke 6:46-49 (page 787).

When we are following God's Word and storms slam into our lives, they will not destroy us! We are living on the indestructible foundation of God. If we are only listening, however, there is only the *appearance* of a foundation beneath us, and we will not withstand the storm.

Read the following verses. Why does God want us to both read and obey His Word?

Matthew 5:16 (page 736)

Titus 2:7 (page 917)

James 2:18 (page 931)

There is a wonderful verse that perfectly describes what God's Word does for us. Read Psalm 19:7 (page 422).

Don't you love it? God's instructions revive our souls. They energize and refresh us. Can you think of a better reason to follow them? And they are absolutely trustworthy. We cannot go wrong following God's instructions. They will not and cannot lead us astray. It's impossible.

> You only really believe that which activates you. Faith is active.

The words *hypocrite* and *Christian* are synonymous to some people today. That's because there are too many Christians who are only hearers of God's Word. Just like James 1:23-24 says, they hear and then immediately "forget" what God wants them to do. A mirror only shows our surface reflection. It does not reflect the heart and soul of the person. Someone who only hears God's Word never gets below the surface to the life-changing truth. God's truth is revealed only as we put His Word into practice and experience it. The word *hypocrite* doesn't apply to someone who is both hearing and doing God's work.

The Problem of the Tongue

James 1:26 (page 930) brings us back to the tongue again.

What connection does it make between religion and our tongue?

Strong words indeed! Our tongue is either our adversary or our ally, but it cannot be both. What can you do to make sure your tongue is your ally?

We must keep looking in the mirror of God's Word to allow Him to show us the sin in our lives. An uncontrolled tongue in a Christian is a terrible thing. Ask for God's help to guard it, control it, and when under trial, be slow to speak. There is an excellent daily prayer we can pray to help maintain control of our tongue.

What does Psalm 141:3 (page 477) say?

Genuine Religion

The first chapter of James ends like it began—on a powerful note. Read James 1:27 (page 930).

What is the focus of *"genuine religion"*?

One theme of the Bible is addressed in this verse. It's addressed more broadly in Philippians 2:3-4 (page 900).

How would you summarize these verses from Philippians?

God did not breathe life into our lungs for us to live for ourselves. Jesus set the example of selflessness for us while He lived on this earth, and now He asks us to follow Him. Let's look at just a few more similar verses:

Matthew 22:37-39 (page 753)

Matthew 5:44 (page 737)

Titus 3:1 (page 918)

Hebrews 12:14 (page 928)

What are your thoughts after reading these verses?

Imagine a world where everyone, both individuals and govern-ments, put these verses into practice. It's impossible, really—the scope is too huge. But imagine a world where *you* put these verses into prac-tice. What would that look like? How would your sphere of influence be impacted? It's not a bad place to start—in fact, it's the *only* place to start. And who knows? Maybe it will catch on.

——————— *Personal Reflection and Application* ———————

From this chapter,

I see...

I believe...

I will...

Prayer

Father, help me live and behave as if I am dead to the power of sin and alive to you through Christ Jesus. Help me to not do as the wicked do, and keep me from following the path of evil-doers. Don't let me even think about it; don't let me go that way. Give me the power to turn away and keep moving (Romans 6:11, page 861, and Proverbs 4:14-15, page 483).

Thoughts, Notes, and Prayer Requests

4

Christian Faith Is Consistent
James 2:1-13

Rushing through my shopping one day, a long list of errands in my hand, I decided to grab something to eat at McDonald's. There were several people in line ahead of me, giving me plenty of observation time. Directly in front of me was a young man whose head was shaved except for a shocking pink fan of hair sticking straight up about four inches high. His baggy black jeans were cut off haphazardly at his knees, and heavy chains looped down from his belt. His ears sported both bores and piercings, and tattoos peeked from beneath his shirt sleeves and collar.

In front of him were two young men about the same age but miles apart culturally. They were dressed in tidy chinos and plaid sport shirts. Their hair was clean and trim, their ears were intact, and their arms had no ink. My eyes flashed back and forth between them, fascinated by the two extremes.

The two young men got up to the counter and ordered hamburgers, fries, and shakes—all double-sized. As they waited for their order I noticed the other young man searching through his pockets. As the two turned around with their laden trays he stared at the food hungrily.

"Can I help you?" the clerk asked coldly.

The boy's face flamed as he looked at the handful of change he'd come up with. "Uh, how much is a Big Mac?"

Sudden compassion washed over me. He was no longer a sight to observe—he was a kid who was hungry. I touched his arm. "Please. Order whatever you want. My treat."

He stared at me wordlessly and then turned and ordered what the boys in front of him had ordered. When he got his food he turned and stared at me again, as if he found my appearance as confounding as I found his. And then he flashed me a shy smile. "Thank you very much," he finally said. "I really appreciate it."

Prayer

Father, you have shown me what real love is because Jesus gave up His life for me. So I also ought to give up my life for my brothers and sisters. If I have enough money to live well and see someone in need but show no compassion toward them—how can your love be in me? Don't let me just say that I love others; let me show the truth by my actions (1 John 3:16-18, page 942).

In the previous chapter, we addressed some tough issues that we deal with every day.

Did you have an opportunity to practice listening rather than speaking? Please share.

Favoritism and Prejudice

Real faith in God always impacts our whole life. It affects our attitude toward Him, others, ourselves, and life in general. In chapter 2 of his letter, James points out some uncomfortable areas, forcing us to face our prejudices. Read James 2:1 (page 930) and note who James was addressing.

James is not writing to people in general. It is specifically to followers of Jesus, who because of their faith in Him are called to a higher level of behavior.

James connects our faith with our behavior. It's because of our faith in God that we behave in a certain way. The way we live should distinguish us from others. In this case James is speaking about how we treat people with favoritism.

How would you define favoritism?

Favoritism is giving unfair preferential treatment to one person or group at the expense of another. This is something we have all been guilty of at one time or another. It is human nature to show favortism but that does not make it right. James goes on to give a typical example of how we show favoritism. Read James 2:2-4 (page 930).

How do you relate to this example? So often we behave like this unconsciously. Can you think of a time you were guilty of similar behavior?

It's just more pleasant to be around certain people, isn't it? But what does James say such discrimination is guided by?

As a follower of Jesus, we should treat every person with dignity and equality. They are all people created in the image of God—He values them enough that Jesus died for them. Let's look at some other places where the Bible addresses favoritism. Read the following verses and note what they say.

Leviticus 19:13-15 (page 94)

2 Chronicles 19:7 (page 345)

1 Timothy 5:21 (page 912)

Strong language was used in all of these verses. God sees discrimination of any kind as sin. He expects us to treat each person with equal respect, regardless of status, wealth, intellectual ability, race, physical appearance, or social acceptability.

Prejudice played a considerable part in the culture we read about in the New Testament. Jewish believers felt they were favored by God because He had blessed them and sent the Savior through their people. Some believed God's salvation was meant only for them, and the Gentiles were excluded.

However, God revealed that mistake to them. We read about it in the tenth chapter of Acts. Cornelius (a Gentile—non-Jew) sent for Peter (one of Jesus' disciples). Cornelius wanted Peter to come and talk to the religious Gentiles who were meeting at his house. Normally Peter would never have responded to such a request, but God revealed to him by way of a vision that he should go. Read Acts 10:28-35 (page 839).

What did Peter see after responding to God's instruction?

Peter's immediate willingness to let go of a strongly ingrained cultural belief is pretty impressive, don't you think? It shows how strong his faith in God was that he immediately did what God asked, in spite of it being against what he had always believed.

How easily do you think you could have done that? Are there some long-held beliefs you've had to struggle with letting go— or that you need to let go of?

Relationship, Not Prejudice

Romans 2:10-11 (page 858) reiterates God's view of prejudice or favoritism. God does not determine a person's value by their economic status, social status, or nationality. He does not accept or reject them based on their career, appearance, or church affiliation. What God desires is that all people be in relationship with Him—a relationship that is found only through Jesus Christ.

While age, talent, office, service, or position often elevate some to a different level in our eyes, we are viewed equally by God. He loves each of us and sent His Son to die for us. The Bible clearly teaches that we should see others through the eyes of Jesus, who crossed many social and ethnic boundaries of His day.

Read the following verses and note some of the boundaries He crossed.

Luke 19:1-7 (page 801)

Mark 1:40-42 (page 762)

John 4:7-9 (pages 811-812)

It's easy to think we don't have prejudices, but everyone does in one way or another. Some typical areas of prejudice we tend not to acknowledge are those toward people with higher or lower financial status, more or less education, higher or lower job positions, and better or worse backgrounds. We can harbor prejudices against people from other religions or ethnic groups or even people who dress differently—such as the young man with the hot-pink hair I met at McDonald's.

We just naturally gravitate toward people of our own culture or social group. But our lives can be greatly enhanced when we reach across these ingrained boundaries, just as Jesus did. Plus, it's what God asks us to do.

Read 1 Peter 2:17 (page 935) and note what it says.

Take a few minutes and think of what prejudices you might be holding that you've not considered. Prejudices can be large, or small—quite hidden. Ask God for two things: to make you aware of your prejudices, and then to bring you opportunities to confront them. As you pray, jot down what comes to mind. This next week watch for the opportunities God brings.

Overcoming prejudices is not easy. It will take courage, determination, and a lot of prayer. But you will be amazed at how God answers your prayer, enabling you to do this and blessing your willingness to change.

The Right Kind of Wealth

James speaks quite strongly about the prejudice between the wealthy and the poor. Read James 2:5-7 (page 931).

What do you think he meant by the poor being rich in faith?

Is it possible that the fewer possessions we have, the more opportunity we have to trust God? One detriment of wealth is the sense of self-sufficiency it can produce. It is very difficult to experience true dependency on God when you can take care of your material needs yourself.

There can be an unhealthy value attached to wealth. People define themselves by their things and often spend their lives trying to accumulate more. Some go so far as to break laws, rob, kill—do whatever it takes to gain more wealth. But think about this: During the three years of His public ministry, Jesus was supported by followers (Luke 8:3, page 788). He rode on a borrowed donkey (Mark 11:2-3, page 772). He ate His last meal in a borrowed room (Mark 14:14, page 775). And He was buried in a tomb owned by someone else (Luke 23:50-53, page 807). In Matthew 8:20 (page 739) He said, *"Foxes have dens to live in, and birds have nests, but the Son of Man has no place even to lay his head."*

Our inclination is to gather all the material things we can in order to feel secure and confident—which may prevent us from finding security and confidence in our relationship with Jesus. Sometimes, what we possess inhibits our faith in God and expands our faith in ourselves.

The only kind of wealth that truly sustains us is internal. Internal wealth comes from faith in God and will provide for us in ways no amount of money and things can.

Read the following verses and note how God has promised to care for all who depend fully on Him:

Isaiah 25:4 (page 535)

Philippians 4:19 (page 901)

Psalm 111:5 (page 466)

Matthew 6:33 (page 738)

2 Corinthians 9:10 (page 886)

There are many more verses that promise God will take care of us. What do the following verses tell us to do?

Mark 12:28-31 (page 773)

1 John 3:23 (page 943)

Philippians 2:3-4 (page 900)

The Law of Love

Read James 2:8-9 (page 931).

According to the final part of these verses, what is favoritism, or prejudice?

What about our attitude must change in order to live out these verses?

There will always be social differences because people have different desires or goals in life and different advantages. But the fact that differences exist does not give us license to break God's law. We should exhibit love and courtesy at all times toward all people.

Now turn to Romans 13:8-10 (page 867).

How do you see love fulfilling the requirements of the law?

What is our obligation?

Have you ever considered love to be an obligation? This takes us back to the action part of faith. Love is not only an emotion we feel for *some* people in our lives. It is also behavior we should exhibit toward *all* people based on a desire to follow Jesus. It causes us to consider our neighbor as we consider ourselves. By doing that we will be fulfilling the requirements of all the other laws, because our actions will always be for the good of the other person as well as ourselves.

It sounds so simple on paper, doesn't it? But putting it into practice is another matter. It does not come naturally to behave in a loving way toward everyone. The auto-focus on our life-lens seems to always revert to self-focus. We respond by categorizing sin, making some sins worse than others, but the law of God is impartial. Read James 2:10-11 (page 931).

It's clear. Anything that breaks God's law puts a barrier between Him and us. In this passage, James compares murder and adultery—but any number of sins can be listed.

Galatians 5:19-21 (page 893) lists a number of areas that put division between us and God. What sins does this passage list?

Any degree of negative behavior toward others is breaking God's law and is viewed the same by Him. Break one and it's the same as breaking them all. It may seem harsh at first, but think about it. If you go to court for a traffic violation, do you plead that you have kept all the other laws? You are a lawbreaker because of your one violation. To disobey God's law in any way is sin.

What does James 2:12 (page 931) say?

If we have believed that Jesus died for our sins and have asked His forgiveness, we are freed from the penalty of death that our sins deserve (Romans 6:23, page 861). This incredible gift from God should bring about a shift in behavior and attitude as we follow the example Jesus set for us while on earth. The Holy Spirit comes to live inside us at the point we receive Jesus, empowering us to live above our natural inclinations. But always we have the choice of following in Jesus' footsteps or following our own selfish nature.

God's Mercy

Read the following verses and note what they say:

2 Corinthians 5:10 (page 884)

Romans 14:11-12 (page 867)

James 2:13 (page 931)

This last verse stops me short! I need and I crave God's mercy, don't you? I want to tack this verse up all over my house and in my car as a continual reminder to treat everyone with mercy.

In Matthew, when Peter asked Jesus about forgiveness, Jesus answered him by telling a story. Read Matthew 18:21-35 (page 749).

Did you notice in verse 27 that the man *completely forgave* the servant's debt? Completely! Just like that the servant was debt free, and his wife and children were saved from the horror of slavery.

Try to imagine what that would feel like. Have you ever had someone write off even a small debt for you? How did you feel?

How did the servant respond?

Incredible! He immediately attacked a man who owed him money. He showed no mercy for him at all. It is such a horrifying story, but think about it for a minute. How many times are we guilty of the same lack of mercy? God brings forgiveness and blessings into our lives in countless ways, and He surrounds us with love, but we continue to live with our well-developed self-focus, giving only token thought to those who need forgiveness and mercy.

What does John 13:35 (page 823) say?

Followers of Jesus should be easily recognized by the love we show each other. How would people around you say your behavior identifies you?

Only the love of God and His transforming power working in us will erase all the forms of prejudice. If we are willing, the Holy Spirit will soften our hearts with compassion and expand our ability to behave in love toward the people around us.

———— *Personal Reflection and Application* ————

From this chapter,

I see…

I believe…

I will…

Prayer

Lord, help me to follow your commandment to love others as you have loved me. I know that there is no greater love than to lay my life down for my friends and that I am your friend when I do what you command. I am so grateful that you call me your friend—and that you chose me and appointed me to produce fruit that will last. Lord, with your help, I will follow your commandment to love others (John 15:12-17, page 824).

Thoughts, Notes, and Prayer Requests

_____

_____

_____

_____

_____

_____

_____

_____

_____

_____

_____

_____

_____

_____

_____

_____

_____

5

Christian Faith Results in Good Works
James 2:14-26

My friend Trina Pockett was taking the ferry to an Alaskan town north of where her family lived. The ferry was very crowded that day, so she and her husband had to split up in order to find seats, each taking one of their children with them. The only two seats Trina could find together were next to a scruffy-looking man with long dark hair who looked like he'd been on the ferry for many days. With some dismay she sat down next to him and set her three-year-old daughter, Kate, beside her.

She handed Kate some crayons to keep her entertained, but after a few minutes of coloring she got distracted. She leaned forward to look around her mom and stared intently at the man sitting next to her. Then she sat back again and commenced coloring. A few minutes later, she again leaned forward and stared long and hard at the man. Trina began to get nervous, sure her daughter was getting ready to say something that would be embarrassing.

When her daughter leaned forward the third time to look at the man she said softly, "Hi, Jesus!"

Oh, for the eyes of a child that see Jesus in the people around us! How differently we might respond. And imagine if people saw Jesus in us! How different our world might look.

Prayer

Lord God, let me love others with the love that comes from you. You showed your love to me by sending your one and only Son into the world so I could have eternal life through Him. Since you loved me, I should also love others. I have never seen you; but if I love others, you live in me and your love is expressed in me. I know and rely on the love you have for me. You are love, and if I live in love, you live in me. I love you because you first loved me. I know that if I claim to love you but hate someone else, it makes me a liar. Because how can I hate someone I've seen but love you, whom I haven't seen? So help me, please, to follow your commandment to love others (1 John 4:7-21, page 943).

We are halfway through the book of James, and as you can see what it may lack in length, it more than makes up for in power. Within this small book is information we need to live the way God wants us to live.

What impact has this study had on your attitude or actions thus far?

Faith and Actions Go Together

Often when we come to the phrase *"dear brothers and sisters,"* we know James is moving onto a new subject.

What does James 2:14 (page 931) say?

James keeps bringing us back to the point that faith and action cannot be separated. You can't have one without the other. James is not talking about the initial step of faith that brings us into relationship with God. He is talking about the result of that faith, which is the response of our hearts to the will of God. Faith demonstrates its presence in our lives by the good things it leads us to do—acts of love, compassion, and kindness. Faith is not just a state of being; it is a state of doing.

Let's look at some other verses about faith.

What is required of us in order to please God according to Hebrews 11:6 (page 926)?

According to John 6:28-29 (page 814), what is the work God requires of us?

What is the result of faith in Romans 5:1 (page 860)?

What does faith do for us in Ephesians 6:16 (page 898)?

What shows our faith in James 2:14,18 (page 931)?

Believing in Jesus is essential to faith. That is the starting point. From then on the result of faith is peace. Our faith protects us, and it motivates us to think and act differently. As our faith grows, so do all these benefits. It's an amazing gift God gives us! And it invariably spills over to the people around us.

Read the following verses and note the importance of our actions to give evidence of our faith:

Matthew 5:16 (page 736)

Ephesians 2:10 (page 896)

1 Timothy 6:18 (page 913)

Titus 3:8 (page 918)

1 John 3:18 (page 942)

Once we have trusted Jesus as Savior and Lord, the emphasis shifts to living out the new life we received as a result of our faith. Just claiming to have faith is not enough. Genuine faith is evidenced by our actions.

It is important that the two, faith and action, do not get switched around in our minds, however. It is not our good actions, doing all the right things, that earn us eternal life with God. There is no amount of being a "good" person that will earn you entrance into heaven.

Faith in Jesus, God's Son, is the only path to eternal life. That faith comes first. The result of that faith is our changed attitude and actions. What do the following verses have to say about this?

Galatians 2:16 (page 891)

Ephesians 2:8-9 (page 896)

Titus 3:4-5 (page 918)

The Bible makes it very clear that we can't earn our way to heaven by being a good person. Eternal life with God is a gift He freely gives us when we believe that Jesus paid the price for our sins by dying on the cross.

Having a Living and Active Faith

Read James 2:15-20 (page 931).

What do you see as the main point of this passage?

Faith is not passive—it is active. It rolls up its sleeves and gets its hands dirty. Faith gets involved with people who need a helping hand.

When we become a follower of Jesus, our lives become a continuing story of fellowship with God and fellowship with people.

But if action results naturally from faith, why do you think James found it necessary to urge us to take action?

Sometimes it's hard to know where to start. Just writing out a check to support organizations who do get involved is an easy way to feel like we're doing something. Certainly the support is important, even vital, but there is nothing that replaces personal involvement. To work side by side, to look into the eyes of someone you're helping—to connect with God and with people by showing them what the love of Jesus is like—this is where faith is lived out.

What are some examples of the *"dead"* faith James talks about?

Sometimes I wonder if telling someone, "Let me know if you need anything," falls into that category. It's responding without responding. I remember visiting a friend once whose husband had just left her for another woman. While I was there, her doorbell rang, and there stood another friend with a dust cloth in one hand and furniture polish in the other. "I'm not here to talk or take up your time," she said. "I'm here to do your dusting." And with that she set to work. My friend sat back down at the table where we were talking, tears streaming down her face, feeling the love of God through that woman's faith in action.

James 2:19 makes a critical point. What does it say?

Believing there is a God is not enough. God wants to have a personal relationship with us and that comes only by believing that He sent His Son, Jesus, to die for our sins. That belief is what transforms our lives, and it's through our transformed lives that a skeptical world learns about Jesus.

Belief is hard to describe because it is intangible and invisible, but it is in living out our belief in God that He is made visible to everyone around us. We bring glory to Him. That's why it is so important that our faith is accompanied by action.

Read James 2:21-24 (page 931).

This incident is recorded in Genesis 22 (page 17). You can read about it later if you like, but it tells about Abraham, a man whose faith and commitment to God was strong and active. Long after giving up hope that they would have a child, his wife, Sarah, miraculously became pregnant. Then God asked the unthinkable of Abraham when He asked him to sacrifice his special son, Isaac. It's an incredible story of how Abraham's faith inspired him to follow God against all logic (Hebrews 11:17-19, page 927).

Abraham was not saved because he obeyed God's command. Instead, this obedience demonstrated that he was already God's child.

James tells us that it was Abraham's *action* that proved his righteousness in God's eyes.

However, Romans 4:1-3 (page 859) shows us the other side of faith. What does it say?

This passage tells us that it was Abraham's *belief* in God that made him righteous. It also says that if he had acted without believing it would have meant nothing. The two simply cannot in any way be separated! Our faith in God is proved by our actions.

Read James 2:25-26 (page 931).

This illustration refers to another incident in Israel's history (Joshua 2:1-24, pages 168-169, and Joshua 6:20-25, page 171). Joshua was leading the people of God into the Promised Land, and he sent out two spies to check out the lay of the land. Unfortunately, they were discovered and forced to run for their lives. They found shelter in the home of Rahab—a prostituted woman—then they were forced to run for their lives. This is an amazing story that is well worth reading when you have time, but the gist of the story is that Rahab's belief in God led her to risk her life by helping the two Israelite spies escape.

Just as in the illustration of Abraham, we see how faith resulted in action and how that action was rewarded by God. Not only was Rahab's life saved, but all of her family was saved when the Israelites conquered the city of Jericho.

Questions to Ask Yourself

In this second chapter, James has clearly shown that our belief in Jesus as our Savior is evidence of our inward faith, which expresses itself in outward action.

As we come to the end of this chapter, here are some questions to think about:

- Which is easier for you—talking about your faith with others or demonstrating love toward them? Why?

- What are some ways you might be able to live out your faith this next week at home? At work? With your friends? With strangers?

- Have you trusted Jesus as your Savior and Lord?

The last question is the most important. If this is something you would like to know more about please turn to the "Know God" section of this study (pages 133–135) for more information.

——————— *Personal Reflection and Application* ———————

From this chapter,

I see…

I believe…

I will…

Prayer

Jesus, you have given me a commandment: Love others. Just as you have loved me, so I must love others. This is how everyone will know I am your follower—by me loving them. So teach me to do your will, because you are my God. May your gracious Spirit lead me forward (John 13:34-35, page 823, and Psalm 143:10, page 478).

Thoughts, Notes, and Prayer Requests

_____

_____

_____

_____

_____

_____

_____

_____

_____

6

Christian Faith Is Shown in Words and Attitudes
James 3:1-18

It was my first time to emcee an event, and I was riding high on an exhilarating wave of success. When the event was over and almost everyone had gone home, a woman approached me. "You don't remember me, do you?" she asked.

I glanced at her name tag, frantically trying to remember, but neither her name nor her face was familiar.

"You wrote me a very rude note five years ago, and I've kept it all this time waiting for the day I'd run into you again."

My mind whirled, trying to remember this woman and what had prompted me to write such a note. Not knowing what else to say, I took her hand and asked her to please forgive me.

It wasn't until that night that all the facts fell into place. I had written the note in defense of a friend who'd been hurt by the woman's words. My motive was right, perhaps, but the action was very wrong. My words had hurt her so much that she'd harbored them for five years.

Oh, the power of the tongue to wound! She'd hurt my friend, I'd hurt her, and now she'd hurt me. The cycle needed to stop—and it did that night when I asked God to forgive me and determined never to repeat such a hurtful action.

Here we go again—being confronted with an unpleasant issue we all have: controlling our tongues! *Ouch!* It would be nice to just glide right over this chapter, but it would not be very beneficial. So we might as well dive right in and see where we land.

Controlling the Tongue: Teaching in the Church

Read James 3:1 (page 931).

How do we know James is again changing the subject?

I smile every time I read that phrase now. It makes James' writing feel very personal.

Why do you think teachers are judged more strictly?

James gave this warning to teachers because some had failed in their responsibilities, adding their personal, unscriptural beliefs to what they taught and living in a way that contradicted their teaching. as evidenced in the following verses:

Acts 15:24 (page 844)

Romans 2:21-23 (page 858)

1 Timothy 1:6-7 (page 910)

2 Timothy 4:3-4 (page 915)

This isn't to discourage us from teaching, but it is to warn us to teach only God's truth and to live the truth we teach. As followers of Jesus we are called to teach in some capacity. Note what the following verses say:

Matthew 28:20 (page 760)

2 Timothy 2:24-25 (page 915)

James 3:2 (page 931) is both a comfort and an understatement.
What does the first part of this verse say?

Aren't you glad that God is aware of and understanding of our
human nature? This verse doesn't just acknowledge that we make mistakes—we *"make many mistakes"*!

That sentence sets a gentle and understanding tone for all the
verses that follow, beginning with the last part of verse 2.

What would happen if we could control our tongues?

If we could control our tongues we would be able to control ourselves *"in every other way"*! Think about that. Our tiny little tongue
wields devastating power. It is actually considered to be the stron-
gest muscle in the body, and it is never bacteria-free. However, this

trouble-causing, germ-infested muscle is also one of our most sensitive muscles and the quickest to heal. Without it, there would be no pleasure in eating, because it is our tongue that delights us with the wide variety and contrast of tastes in this world.

Controlling the Tongue: The Power of Our Words

James 3:3-5 (page 931) compares the strength of our tongues to three different things.

As you read this passage, list the items below.

How often in politics have we witnessed a career brought down by thoughtless words? How often have malicious rumors destroyed a leader, a relationship, or a dream? Read the following passages and note what they say about the tongue:

James 3:6-8 (page 931)

Proverbs 18:21 (page 494)

The description of our tongues is shockingly harsh. That last phrase is the worst— *"Those who love to talk will reap the consequences."* Does it make you want to clamp on a muzzle and never utter another word?

Why do you think it is so difficult to tame the tongue?

The tongue reveals our inner person. The outlet for our thoughts is usually our tongue.

When we speak, it can reveal everything from the country or region we are from to our personal interests. It can also reveal our character and our spiritual condition. Matthew 12:34b-35 (page 743) talks about this when it says, *"Whatever is in your heart determines what you say. A good person produces good things from the treasury of a good heart, and an evil person produces evil things from the treasury of an evil heart."*

The most devastating aspect of our words is that they cannot be taken back. Even if we didn't mean them—and no matter how much we apologize—the words may remain in the mind of the person you spoke to.

Have you ever said something that you know someone else still remembers?

Yes, our words are powerful, but God's forgiveness is greater. Take a moment and pray this Scripture together:

Take control of what I say, O LORD, and guard my lips.
Don't let me drift toward evil or take part in acts of wickedness.

Psalm 141:3-4a (page 477)

Controlling the Tongue: The Source of Our Speech

Read James 3:9-12 (page 931).

Think about the logic of this passage for a moment. Bitter water and fresh water do come from entirely different sources, olives and figs from far different plants. How then can we speak words of praise to God one moment and yell at someone the next, when such words come from entirely different attitudes?

We can be thankful that as followers of Christ we are connected to Him like a branch is to a vine. Jesus taught about this in John 15:1-17 (page 824). Because of this connection to Christ, we have access to His power that produces good fruit in our lives. Apart from Him, we can do nothing. But when His power is working in us, our lives will produce fruit that will last.

The more we gain control of our tongue, the more blessing we will receive as a result of our words.

Can you think of an example of how someone's good words blessed you recently?

God is not telling us to stop talking, but to talk about the right things and in the right way.

Read Philippians 4:8 (page 901) for some helpful advice.

Two Kinds of Wisdom

The remaining verses in James 3 have to do with two different kinds of wisdom. Read James 3:13-18 (page 931).

As you read, note the two kinds of wisdom and the characteristics of each.

What a contrast between the two lists! Keeping these lists in mind, look up the following passages, and note what they say about wisdom:

Proverbs 2:6-7 (page 482)

Proverbs 3:13-14 (page 482)

God will give us *a treasure of common sense* as we cultivate His wisdom. He will give us joy and understanding! It's the exact opposite of disorder, lying, and selfish ambition. One way is superbly beneficial and one is highly destructive.

People who have bitter jealousy or selfish ambition in their hearts usually are not able to share true wisdom, but rather a counterfeit type of wisdom which is not God-given but worldly. It results in disorder, all kinds of evil, and confusion. God is not the author of confusion but of peace.

What does 1 Corinthians 1:30 (pages 870-871) say about wisdom?

It's an amazing, incredible thing God has done for us. Jesus, our Wisdom, died for our sins so we could be right with God. When we ask Him to forgive our sins, then we become pure and holy in God's eyes (1 John 1:7, page 941). He does not see any of our sins, and we have access to His wisdom—because the Holy Spirit now lives within us.

As believers, we are pure because God has cleansed us. However, we are surrounded by opportunities to make wrong choices, and our sinful natures sometimes give in to temptation. We need the continual cleansing that only comes through our relationship with Jesus as we confess our sins to Him. He will always forgive us (1 John 1:9, page 941).

James 3:17 lists several characteristics of the wisdom we get from God. How is wisdom described?

Living up to these characteristics of godly wisdom is not a small challenge, but do you remember what we learned about wisdom in James 1:5 (page 930)?

Are you lacking in godly wisdom? Just ask God for it! He gives us wisdom in a variety of ways—through Bible study, prayer, sound biblical teaching, time spent with spiritually mature Christians, and godly books, and as we follow His guidance given to us through the Holy Spirit.

> What does James 3:18 (page 931) tell us will be the result of true spiritual wisdom?

Would you love to be described as someone who *"plants seeds of peace"* wherever you go? Wouldn't you love to always be reaping *"a harvest of righteousness"*?

The result of true spiritual wisdom is a life that reflects the life of Jesus. Godly wisdom preserves unity and peace. It enables us to be a help rather than a hindrance. Wisdom selects the highest goals and uses the best means of reaching them. Wisdom cannot be separated from goodness or gentleness or mercy, or any of the other characteristics we've considered. This week, ask God each day to fill you with His wisdom. Next week we can share the results we experienced.

———— *Personal Reflection and Application* ————

From this chapter,

I see…

I believe…

I will…

Prayer

Lord, help me to not turn my back on wisdom, for it is my protection. Help me to love wisdom so it will guard me. I know that getting wisdom is the wisest thing I can do! So help me above all else to develop good judgment. Don't let me ever be impressed with my own wisdom; may I always fear you and turn away from evil. I understand that the fear of the Lord is true wisdom and to forsake evil is real understanding (Proverbs 4:6-7, page 483; Proverbs 3:7, page 482; Job 28:28, page 405).

Thoughts, Notes, and Prayer Requests

7

Christian Faith Results in Humility
James 4:1-17

A business consultant was in line to check his luggage at JFK Airport in New York. The man in front of him was angry and rude to the airline clerk helping him. The consultant was impressed by how the clerk handled the man. He remained calm and courteous in response to the angry passenger. When the consultant got up to the clerk, he complimented him on how well he had handled the difficult customer.

"That was the most unreasonable fellow I've seen in a long time," he told him. "I'm a management consultant and would like to tell your story in one of my seminars. May I ask what training your company gives that enables you to control yourself when someone is so obnoxious?"

The clerk looked at him without expression. "We don't get trained in stuff like that," he said. "They just tell us never to blow up at a customer, so I don't. Of course, that guy is going to Chicago and his bags are going to Singapore."[3]

It's a good story to keep in mind the next time you're tempted to speak your mind. There is a right way and wrong way to respond to frustrating circumstances, which is what chapter 4 of James is all about. I think you'll enjoy this chapter, but get ready to have your toes stepped on!

Prayer

Lord, your Word tells me that sensible people control their temper and earn respect by overlooking wrongs. Help me to have understanding and control my anger, because I know a hot temper shows great foolishness. I want to be wise and cautious and avoid danger, rather than be a fool who plunges ahead with reckless confidence. Protect me from a short temper that causes me to do foolish things (Proverbs 19:11, page 494; Proverbs 14:29, page 491; Proverbs 14:16-17, page 490).

The book of James is like a handbook for good life practices. Follow the principles within this book and you'll find your relationships improving, as well as the quality of your life. In this book, God, the real Author, reveals His thoughts about everyday behavior. As we've already seen, James speaks very candidly. He doesn't soft-pedal any subject. Chapter 4 continues in his same plain-speaking style.

The last verse of chapter 3 talked about peacemakers. Well, chapter 4 starts out with the opposite behavior. It begins by asking, *"What is causing the quarrels and fights among you?"*

Chapter 3 compared the characteristics of the wisdom that comes from God with the wisdom that comes from the world.

What were some of the characteristics resulting from the world's wisdom?

Now in chapter 4 we'll see that these characteristics lead to bad and destructive behavior. If there is anger within us, it will ultimately lead to anger around us. People have a tendency to respond in a similar way to how they are treated. And it is impossible to be at peace with others unless we are at peace within ourselves.

Why do you think there is so much quarreling and hatred in the world today?

Desires and Conflict

James 4:1-3 (page 932) answers the question we just asked.

What are the reasons it gives?

Much of the global unrest today is caused by desire for power, position, and possessions along with a refusal to acknowledge God. Think about it. What has been at the heart of governments that have collapsed? Corrupt leadership. What causes a leader to become corrupt? Self-focused attitudes. What is at the heart of marriages that collapse? A self-focused attitude on the part of one or both spouses. What is at the root of the debt that has a stranglehold on both individuals and governments? Wanting what we do not have.

Such evil was a problem way back in the first century, and it is still a problem now. Almost all failures can be traced back to an attitude that is turned inward, focusing on self rather than on others and on God.

Our desires seem reasonable and harmless, and many of them are—until we decide to have them before we can afford them or to have them at someone else's expense. That's where the trouble begins.

The last part of verse 2 and all of verse 3 are profound. Why do they say we don't have what we want?

Talk about oversimplifying. That surely sounds like what James is doing here, but he really isn't. In verse 3, why does he say we don't get what we want?

If all of our desires are centered around what will bring us pleasure, what will the result be?

Pleasure is insatiable. It always wants a little more—until we are consumed by wanting a little more and are discontent because we don't have it. Only when we find a way to pull our focus off the external and turn it to the internal will we experience a life honoring to God and satisfying to us. When we are led by the Holy Spirit and our motives are pure, God hears our requests. He will answer us because our heart's desire matches His heart's desire.

It's easy to get mixed up in this area, thinking our motives are pure when we pray for something. For example, what if you were being considered for a promotion? You start to pray fervently that God will give you the promotion, because it might enable you to care for your family better or give more to Him, which are both good-sounding motives. But when someone else is promoted instead, you've set yourself up to feel betrayed. Yet God never betrays us. Faith is trusting that He knows what is best. Faith is believing His promise to take care of all your needs. Faith understands that your circumstances are in no way dependent on the promotion but on Him.

Sometimes we get distracted by what sounds like a solution to us. We put faith in how the promotion would provide better for us, rather than in how God will provide. It's a subconscious skewing of motive that He sees more clearly than we do. Through our circumstances He is always working to bring us into a closer, more trusting, and more dependent relationship with Him. Faith says, "This opportunity looks good to me, God, but I want only what will draw me closer to you." That kind of sincere prayer will filter out our selfish motives.

> Can you think of a time when you prayed for something God didn't give you and later you saw it was for the best? Please share.

If we set our priorities around pleasure, wealth, or position, satisfaction will always be just beyond our fingertips. We will always be grasping for what eludes us. That doesn't make for a satisfying, fulfilled life. Lasting satisfaction is impossible apart from God. When our desires are in line with His desires, He will be glorified, and we will be satisfied.

Divided Loyalties

Read James 4:4-6 (page 932).

James uses strong language here—even calling the people adulterers. But when you consider that God wants to be in relationship with us, that He wants our whole heart, then it makes sense. Adulterers try to have it both ways. They want to be in relationship with their spouse and with another person at the same time. It just doesn't work, as anyone who has been in that position will tell you. It's going to make an enemy out of your spouse. It is the same with our spiritual relationship with God. God wants all of our attention and focus. Exodus 34:14 (page 72) tells us that God is jealous for our relationship with Him.

What do the following verses say about how we should respond to the world?

James 1:27 (page 930)

Galatians 6:14 (page 894)

Philippians 2:15 (page 900)

Titus 2:12 (page 917)

Romans 12:2 (page 866)

1 John 2:15-17 (page 942)

The world system is operating on principles that are opposed to God in many ways—principles of force, greed, ambition, and pleasure. What it honors, what attracts us to it, is of little value.

In the last passage, what did it say the world has to offer?

A Love Relationship with God

Read James 4:4-6 (page 932) again.

This is again talking about our love relationship with God. The Bible often talks about God's love for us being jealous. I love how *The Message* paraphrases James 4:4.

> *You're cheating on God. If all you want is your own way, flirting with the world every chance you get, you end up enemies of God and his way. And do you suppose God doesn't care? The proverb has it that "he's a fiercely jealous lover." And what he gives in love is far better than anything else you'll find. It's common knowledge that "God goes against the willful proud; God gives grace to the willing humble."*

It is human nature to want success and security by the world's standards, but God's grace—His undeserved help—is even stronger and will enable us to overcome the strong pull of the world. God's grace is greater than any sin, any weaknesses, and any spiritual conflict. He is always giving us more grace (Hebrews 4:16, page 922).

According to James 4: 6, who does God oppose and who does He favor?

Pride distracts us from God. It gets in the way of our love relationship with Him. No wonder God opposes the proud. But humility sets the stage for us to receive the grace God has for us.

What is at the core of how we are to draw near to God?

Staying Close to God

God shows us how to access the life He offers us in James 4:7-10 (page 932).

Why do you think humility is so vital to our relationship with God?

An attitude of humility recognizes the Lordship of Christ and the sovereignty of God. It recognizes that He is our Creator and everything we have comes from Him. It understands that He is the only dependable source of peace and security. An attitude of humility says, *God, I want your way, not mine.*

Let's look at James 4:7 again. What does it say will happen when we resist the devil?

Oh, I love the picture this paints. The devil flees. He doesn't just shrug and walk away. He flees! Think about that for a moment. What causes someone to flee?

The devil is terrified of God's power, and when we resist him he recognizes God's power in us. He knows he is no match for that power. Do you see the level of safety we have when we draw near to God?

The contrasting pictures in the end of verse 7 and the beginning of verse 8 are incredible. The devil flees and God comes close. Close your eyes and see yourself turning in God's direction and reaching your hands out to Him. As you do this, see a cloud of dust behind you, caused by the devil's flight away from you. Then imagine God sweeping you up into His arms. Lock that picture in your mind.

What impact does this image have on your life right now?

What are some ways you can not only come close to God, but stay close to Him?

The Bible tells us how to resist the devil. Read the following verses:

1 Peter 5:8-9 (page 937)

Ephesians 6:10-18 (page 898)

Jesus showed us how to resist the devil when He Himself was tempted by the devil on earth. Read Luke 4:1-13 (page 783).

How did Jesus respond to each temptation?

Knowing what the Bible says is a sure defense against the devil's temptations. He cannot deceive you if you know God's Word. We also have the Holy Spirit working in and through us, giving us the strength and ability to live for God. Read Romans 8:5-14 (page 862).

"All who are led by the Spirit of God are children of God." What a wonderful assurance of our relationship to God when we walk through life with the help of the Holy Spirit. It takes humility, though, to put aside our own plans and take the extra time to listen for the Spirit's guiding in our lives. But as we listen and follow, the Holy Spirit will guide us away from sin and toward actions and thoughts that will make us more like Christ.

Interference from Sin

When we resist humility, we fall into sin, whether it's pride or another sin that results from our pride.

Read the following verses to see what our attitude and action should be after we choose to sin.

James 4:9-10 (page 932)

Psalm 51:1-2 (page 436)

2 Corinthians 7:1 (page 885)

Sin is serious. It separates us from God. A little lie that has a little effect and a devastating lie that brings down a life are both sin.

Sin gets in the way of our conversations and our relationship with God. Read Psalm 66:18 (page 442).

What can hinder our prayers?

Our sin can impede our prayers! God wants our relationship to be free of interferences that distract us from His love. God wants us to delight in Him as He delights in us.

Humility with God

James 4:10 again brings up the importance of an attitude of humility, but this time it is connected to a promise.

What is the promise?

Is that hard for you to fathom—that God *"will lift you up in honor"*? When we come humbly asking for forgiveness, God will forgive and lift us up—because of His grace and love for us.

The apostle Paul gave an example of true humility when he said in 1 Corinthians 15:9 (page 879), *"I am the least of all the apostles,"* and in Ephesians 3:8 (page 896) when he said, *"I am the least deserving of all God's people."*

In spite of all Paul did as a servant of Jesus, he never ceased to be aware of the fact that his service was nothing compared to what Jesus had done for him when He died on the cross for Paul's sins. That same awareness should always be at the forefront of our minds, spurring us on to be an accurate reflection of Jesus.

Some people depend on God fully when they first become a Christian, but then fall back to living more and more independently of Him.

Have you noticed your relationship with God change since you became a believer? What do you think caused that change?

We will never reach a level in our relationship with God where we will not need Him. The more aware we are of our need, the stronger our relationship will be.

Judging and Criticizing

In the next two verses, James again hits a nerve. Read James 4:11-12 (page 932).

What does James instruct us not to do?

What does it say we are actually criticizing and judging?

It is no small thing when we criticize or judge someone—or speak evil of them. When was the last time you were guilty of this?

If you're like me, it was probably quite recently. Sadly, it's often those closest to us we are most likely to criticize. I've never forgotten something my husband said to me not long after we were married. He was helping me with the dishes, but was not being as thorough as I thought he should be. Finally he looked at me and said, "Jan, it is easier to criticize than try to understand." His words are imprinted on my brain, and they have been an uncomfortable monitor every time critical words come to mind.

Jesus had some pretty strong words about judging others. Read what He said in Matthew 7:1-5 (page 738).

We are all guilty of judging at one time or another. Sometimes it is subconscious and sometimes it is deliberate, but it is never good and we should be on guard against it.

How will God judge us, according to Matthew 7:2?

It is certainly fair, but it is surely not the way I want God to judge me. If I want His mercy, not His judgment, I'd better start working on my mercy skills!

Not being judgmental does *not* mean ignoring evil. As followers of Jesus, we are to uphold what is good and abhor what is not. We are to tell right from wrong and work against wrong. That's how we bring light to our world.

In what ways can we stand against evil without being judgmental?

Read 1 Corinthians 4:5 (page 872) and note what it says about judging.

Let God be the judge of people. Our attitude toward people should be one of love.

Leave the Future with God

Read James 4:13-16 (page 932).

What attitude should we have in regard to our future?

We have no guarantee of tomorrow—we have no guarantee of the next minute! You may have known someone whose life ended without warning or someone whose life was changed in a minute. My stepsister, fresh out of college with the world at her feet, was hit by a drunk driver and was left severely brain-injured. One second changed all of our lives.

What this passage brings us back to is the importance of humility—acknowledging that only God is truly in control and then relinquishing to Him our need to control. Every second of our lives is in His hands.

> Proverbs 27:1 (page 500) talks about the very same thing. What does it say?

Now we come to the last verse of James chapter 4—the perfect end for this chapter. Read James 4:17 (page 932).

Through the words of James, God is helping us know better so we can do better. He wants us to live well. Therefore, we each have a responsibility to obey what He has revealed. If we make no attempt to obey, we have sinned against Him. An important truth to remember from this lesson is that responsibility accompanies knowledge.

Personal Reflection and Application

From this chapter,

I see…

I believe…

I will…

Prayer

God, I know that despite all these things, overwhelming victory is mine through Christ, who loves me. You have convinced me that nothing can ever separate me from your love. Neither death nor life, neither angels nor demons, neither my fears for today nor my worries about tomorrow—not even the powers of hell can separate me from your love. No power in the sky above or in the earth below—indeed, nothing in all creation will ever be able to separate me from your love that is revealed in Christ Jesus my Lord. Even though I do not see Christ yet, I trust Him, and I rejoice with a glorious, inexpressible joy (Romans 8:37-39, page 863, and 1 Peter 1:8, page 934).

Thoughts, Notes, and Prayer Requests

8

Christian Faith Is Victorious
James 5:1-20

In her book *Seeing God in the Simple Things*, Katherine Weaver tells about one afternoon when her daughter was finger painting. Marie was having a marvelous time, swirling the vibrant colors all across the paper. The more she mixed the colors, the more they changed. The blues and yellows were transformed into greens, the reds and blues into purple. She turned to look at Katherine, who was watching her.

"How's it going?" Katherine asked her.

"It may not look like it right now, Mom," Marie said, "but I'm making something beautiful!"[4]

I think perhaps that is what God might say to us about the picture being painted of our life. When we question the dark mix of colors that come from pain, the muted mix of colors when nothing seems to be happening, I think God, the ultimate Artist, would smile over the work in progress that is us and say, "It may not look like it right now, but I'm making something beautiful!"

That's what faith is all about—trusting the expertise of the Artist and allowing His fingers to swirl through our lives in a way He knows will result in exquisite beauty.

Prayer

Lord, I know that it is better to take refuge in you than to trust in people. You are my rock, my fortress, and my savior in whom I find protection. You are my shield, the power that saves me, and my place of safety. Your way is perfect. All your promises prove true. You are worthy, O Lord my God, to receive glory and honor and power. For you created all things, and they exist because you created what you pleased (Psalm 118:8, page 468; Psalm 18:2, page 420; 2 Samuel 22:31a, page 254; and Revelation 4:11, page 952).

And now we come to the final chapter of James.

What have you learned so far from this study? What do you plan to implement into your life?

This small book written by James deals with many life issues that cause us trouble: not backing our faith up with action, not controlling what we say, harboring prejudices, being critical, being judgmental, and so on. They are all covered in this book, along with instruction on how to avoid these common pitfalls. Our relationships with family members, with our community, and with co-workers would be vastly different if we lived by the principles found in this book.

Trusting in Wealth Undermines Faith

Each chapter has tackled incendiary topics head-on, and this last chapter is no exception. James chooses to write to Christians who are rich in wealth and material goods. Read James 5:1-6 (page 932).

What is the picture James paints of these people?

It's one of complete self-involvement and independence. It is also one of great tragedy because they have put all their trust in stuff that rots away. All that they have accumulated, sometimes at the expense of others, will be gone in a moment and they will be facing an eternity with nothing left.

What do the following passages say about this?

1 Timothy 6:7 (page 912)

Psalm 49:10 (page 435)

The inclination to trust in our ability to provide for ourselves is a common trap for Christians. Regardless of whether we are wealthy or not, there is an inner urge to protect ourselves by building up our bank accounts and accumulating belongings. There is an undeniable allure to the feeling of getting ahead, and it can very subtly erode our faith in God as it captures more of our time and attention, leaving less for God.

What does 1Timothy 6:10 (page 913) say about this?

If you look again at James 5:1-6 you'll see that it isn't critical of being wealthy. There's nothing wrong with wealth. Rather it's the attitude, focus, and misuse of wealth—it is these things that come between people of wealth and their relationship with God.

Read 1 John 2:17 (page 942).

This is what we need to always remember. This world and all the things in it we crave are only temporary. It will eventually all come to an end. And no matter how hard we have worked, or what we have gathered around us, not one speck of it will go with us into eternity. Even if we could take it with us, the most magnificent possession on this earth, the hugest accumulation of wealth, would be like a few pennies in comparison to the wonders of heaven.

All of our money belongs to God. To base our security in anything but Him is delusional. Our wealth and possessions, however small or large, should be placed in endeavors that bring glory to Him. If you can give your money away easily, then you know you own your money rather than your money owning you. The opposite is what you must guard against.

Again, James is not teaching that it is wrong to have assets, but it is wrong to allow them to interfere with our faith and our dependence on God.

Wealth That Comes from God

Read the following verses and note the various "aspects of wealth" that come from God:

Ephesians 3:16 (page 896)

1 Timothy 1:14 (page 910)

Titus 3:6-7 (page 918)

What do all these things have in common?

They do not wear out, rust out, or rot out. These all have eternal worth and vastly enrich our lives—far more than our material wealth ever can.

According to Matthew 6:20-21 (page 737), how safe is our trust in spiritual wealth?

What does 1 Chronicles 29:11-12 (page 332) say about the source of material wealth?

Patience During Difficult Times

Remember that James is writing primarily to Jewish Christians, who are experiencing difficult times as a result of their belief in Jesus. But everything he says to them is still amazingly applicable to us today.

Read James 5:7-9 (page 932) and note what James is telling his hearers.

Patience is not a natural trait of the average human. We want to take the shortcut and try to bypass the hard parts. When pain and heartache are involved, patience can be agonizing.

What situation in your life currently requires patience?

For the believers of James' day, life had become one injustice and persecution after another. They were eager for Jesus to return and correct the wrongs they were suffering. They knew there would be no injustices in the judgment He would bring with His return. Isaiah

11:3-5 (pages 525-526) talks about when Jesus returns. As you read this passage, note the aspects of His judgment.

God's judgment is incorruptible. He can only be righteous, just, and fair. He judges by truth, and He has all the facts. If you are a follower of Jesus, you have nothing to fear. Whatever injustice you have suffered here on earth He will make up for. No evil act will escape His wrath. This is why we can be patient even as we suffer. Our loving God will eventually make it up to us, and He will reward our patience.

What advice do the following verses give us about taking matters into our own hands?

Romans 12:19 (page 866)

Psalm 27:14 (page 425)

Psalm 37:7 (page 429)

What concepts do these verses talk about?

Patience is tied to self-restraint. When we cultivate patience while keeping our focus on God, the desire to retaliate will not take root. We will feel peace even when turmoil swirls around us. Patience is a large part of faith. It proves our trust in God—that we know we can count on Him to do the right thing at the right time.

What examples of patience are given in James 5:7,10-11 (page 932)?

Each example represents a lot of patience. The farmers' patience is cultivated by looking forward to the harvest. The prophets' patience was cultivated by waiting for the judgment and mercy of God. Looking forward to Jesus' return is what we can attach our patience to. It is why we face the challenges of life on earth, knowing He will reward our patient endurance with something too wonderful to comprehend—eternal life with Him in heaven.

The reference to Job is a reminder that sometimes God rewards our faithful endurance in this life as well. Job suffered greatly during one period of his life, and yet he remained focused on God, trusting Him in the midst of his agony.

What does verse 11 say about how God treated Job?

Read Job 42:12-17 (page 414) to see the definition of God's "kindness" to Job.

Not all believers receive earthly recompense as Job did, but God's eternal recompense for faithful endurance and patience is sure. He loves to bless His faithful followers.

What do you think is meant by the instruction in James 5:12 (page 932)?

As followers of Christ, we should always live in a way that our word is impeccable. Our reputation should be such that nothing is needed to back up our word. People should never have to worry about the "hidden message" behind what we say.

This verse is not referring to times when the law requires us to take an oath, such as before a judge. It is talking about being utterly trustworthy in all our business, family, and other relationships.

Prayer and Faith

The last part of chapter 5 talks about prayer, which is an essential element in our relationship with Jesus. Read James 5:13-15 (page 932).

What reasons does it give us for praying?

Don't you love the "*Are any of you happy? You should sing praises*" part? Praying when we're happy is as important as praying when we're troubled. Everything is a reason for prayer, because prayer is how we communicate with God. He wants to hear our voices calling out to Him and singing praises to Him.

Verses 14 and 15 are often misunderstood. What does verse 14 tell us to do?

In the Bible, oil almost always refers to olive oil, which served many purposes. You may remember in the story of the Good Samaritan (Luke 10:33-34, page 792), when he found the man who had been beaten by bandits, it says he *"soothed his wounds with olive oil and wine and bandaged them."* Olive oil was also mixed with spices and perfumes and used as a sacred anointing oil, such as when Samuel anointed David as the next king of Israel (1 Samuel 16:13, page 223). In the Bible, anointing someone with oil was used both ceremonially and medicinally.

Today, some people use oil when praying for healing. The important point of this verse, however, is that it is the prayer of faith to God that truly matters, not the oil.

What does verse 15 imply about faith?

Although sometimes sickness is the result of personal sin, some people feel this verse connects all illnesses to sin. If you are healthy, it is because you are sinless; and if you are sick, it is a result of sin in your life. Others believe that if you pray for healing and are not healed, it is because you do not have enough faith. Such ideas have caused needless pain for people who are already suffering.

Faith is especially vital when going through times of illness, not for the purpose of healing as much as for recognizing the sovereignty of God who has allowed the illness to occur.

Verse 15 says, *"The Lord will make you well."* God is always able to heal, but the truth is, He doesn't always do it. A good example of His not healing someone is the apostle Paul. He was a man of great faith, a selfless, committed servant of Jesus whose prayer for healing was not answered. Read 2 Corinthians 12:8-10 (page 888).

God's purpose in not healing Paul was so he would experience the sufficiency of God's grace for any circumstance. God wanted Paul and others to see His power working through Paul's weakness.

> The beautiful part of this passage is Paul's response to God's not healing him. How did Paul respond?

He *boasted* in his weakness and took *pleasure* in his suffering because it provided a means for God's power to be displayed in his life!

In contrast to Paul's faith-filled prayer for healing that was denied is the story of Naaman in 2 Kings 5:1-16 (page 286).

What a great story! Naaman didn't even believe in God. He went to the prophet surrounded by all the symbols of human power. He was filled with arrogance and pride, even though he suffered from an awful disease. *And yet God healed him!*

The sovereignty of God cannot be explained. Our finite minds cannot grasp His infinite mind. We do not see or know what He knows. What we do know, however, is that He loved us enough to send His Son, Jesus, to die for our sins so that we could have a personal relationship with Him now on earth and eternal life in heaven. He sacrificed everything to make that happen. The least we can do is trust His love when our prayers are not answered in the way we want.

Read James 5:16-18 (pages 932-933).

Verse 16 is a wonderful picture of how followers of Jesus are to support each other and the result of that support. As we share our struggles with each other, we can pray for each other to become stronger and more like Jesus.

> What does verse 16 say about these prayers we pray for others?

God wants us to come to Him with any and all situations—sickness, salvation, whatever. We have the Holy Spirit in us, directing us to pray as He leads. That is where the power comes from! That is what makes our prayers effective! Let's look at the example of Elijah's prayer in 1 Kings 17:1 (page 275) and 18:41-45 (page 277).

I love the picture painted in 1 Kings 18. It clearly shows that Elijah was indeed human, just like us. He boldly told King Ahab it was going to rain, but then as he prayed you can almost feel the doubts growing each time he sent the servant out to check for clouds. Seven times he sent him out!

> Can you remember a time when you prayed desperately for something, like Elijah did, terrified that God would not come through?

> After his seventh cloud-scouting trip the servant reports one little cloud—*"about the size of a man's hand"*—but it was all Elijah needed. What did he have his servant tell Ahab?

One minuscule cloud and he prepares for a torrential downpour! And this is the example God gives us to show us the power our prayers unleash!

Supporting Each Other

And here we are now, at the final two verses of our study of James. Read James 5:19-20 (page 933).

Just as verse 16 showed the importance of supporting each other as we follow in the footsteps of Jesus, so do these final two verses. When we see someone drifting away from their commitment, as God directs us we should do everything we can to bring them back.

> Can you remember a time when your commitment to God was faltering and someone came alongside you? How did they help you?
>
>
>
> We need each other to keep our faith vibrant and growing. We need each other's encouragement to keep doing the right things. What does Hebrew 10:24-25 (page 926) say?

Think about that! How wonderful if we were always motivating each other *"to acts of love and good works."* It would be so much easier, wouldn't it? The truth is, we need each other. It is how God created us—to be in community with each other, and most especially with Him.

Do you know what it means to have a personal relationship with God? It is what He desires for you above all else. If you want to know more about this, turn to the "Know God" section on pages 133–135. This is the most important decision you will ever make, and I am praying for you as you consider it.

In closing, what concept in this study has had the greatest impact on you?

I'm so glad you were a part of this study. I hope it has been a blessing to you, and I hope we meet again in another study!

———— *Personal Reflection and Application* ————

From this chapter,

I see...

I believe...

I will...

Prayer

God, your unfailing love is better than life itself; how I praise you! I will praise you as long as I live, lifting up my hands to you in prayer. You satisfy me more than the richest feast. I will praise you with songs of joy (Psalm 63:3-5, page 441).

Thoughts, Notes, and Prayer Requests

_____

_____

_____

_____

_____

_____

_____

_____

_____

_____

_____

_____

_____

_____

Journal Pages

_____

_____

_____

_____

_____

_____

_____

_____

_____

_____

_____

_____

_____

_____

_____

_____

_____

_____

_____

Know God

It does not matter what has happened in your past. No matter what you've done, no matter how you've lived your life,

God is personally interested in you right now.
He cares about you.

God understands your frustration, your loneliness, your heartaches. He wants each of us to come to Him, to know Him personally.

God is so rich in mercy, and he loved us so much,
that even though we were dead because of our sins,
he gave us life when he raised Christ from the dead.
(It is only by God's grace that you have been saved!)
—*Ephesians 2:4-5 (page 895)*

God loves you.

He created you in His image. His desire is to be in relationship with you. He wants you to belong to Him.

Sadly, our sin gets in the way. It separates us from God, and without Him we are dead in our spirits. There is nothing we can do to close that gap. There is nothing we can do to give ourselves life. No matter how well we may behave.

But God loves us so much that He made a way to eliminate that gap and give us new life, His kind of life—to restore the relationship. His love for us is so great, so tremendous, that He sent Jesus Christ, His only Son, to earth to live, and then die—filling the gap and taking the punishment we deserve for refusing God's ways.

God made Christ, who never sinned,
to be the offering for our sin,
so that we could be made right with God through Christ.
—*2 Corinthians 5:21 (page 884)*

Jesus Christ, God's Son, not only died to pay the penalty for your sin, but He conquered death when He rose from the grave. He is ready to share His life with you.

Christ reconciles us to God. Jesus is alive today. He will give you a new beginning and a newly created life when you surrender control of your life to Him.

Anyone who belongs to Christ has become a new person.
The old life is gone; a new life has begun!
—*2 Corinthians 5:17 (page 884)*

How do you begin this new life? You need to realize

…the necessity of repenting from sin and turning to God,
and of having faith in our Lord Jesus.
—*Acts 20:21 (page 849)*

Agree with God about your sins and believe that Jesus came to save you, that He is your Savior and Lord. Ask Him to lead your life.

God loved the world so much that he gave his one
and only Son, so that everyone who believes in him
will not perish but have eternal life.
God sent his Son into the world not to judge the world,
but to save the world through him.

—*John 3:16-17 (page 811)*

Pray something like this:

Jesus, I do believe you are the Son of God and that you died on the cross to pay the penalty for my sin. Forgive me. I turn away from my sin and choose to life a life that pleases you. Enter my life as my Savior and Lord.

I want to follow you and make you the leader of my life.

Thank you for your gift of eternal life and for the Holy Spirit, who has now come to live in me. I ask this in your name. Amen.

God puts His Spirit inside you, who enables you to live a life pleasing to Him. He gives you new life that will never die, that will last forever—eternally.

When you surrender your life to Jesus Christ, you are making the most important decision of your life. Stonecroft would like to offer you a free download of *A New Beginning*, a short Bible study that will help you as you begin your new life in Christ. Go to **stonecroft.org/ newbeginning**.

If you'd like to talk with someone right now about this prayer, call **1.888.NEED.HIM.**

Who Is Stonecroft?

Every day Stonecroft communicates the Gospel in meaningful ways. Whether side by side with a neighbor or new friend, or through a speaker sharing her transformational story, the Gospel of Jesus Christ goes forward. Through a variety of outreach activities and small group Bible studies specifically designed for those not familiar with God, and with online and print resources focused on evangelism, Stonecroft proclaims the Gospel of Jesus Christ to women where they are, as they are.

For more than 75 years, always with a foundation of prayer in reliance on God, Stonecroft volunteers have found ways to introduce women to Jesus Christ and train them to share His Good News with others.

Stonecroft understands and appreciates the influence of one woman's life. When you reach her, you touch everyone she knows—her family, friends, neighbors, and co-workers. The real Truth of the Gospel brings real redemption into real lives.

Our life-changing, faith-building community resources include:

- *Stonecroft Bible and Book Studies*—both topical and chapter-by-chapter studies. We designed Stonecroft studies for those in small groups—those who know Christ and those who do not yet know Him—to simply yet profoundly discover God's Word together.

- ***Stonecroft Prays!***—calls small groups of women together to pray for God to show them avenues to reach women in their community with the Gospel.

- ***Outreach Events***—set the stage for women to hear and share the Gospel with their communities. Whether in a large venue, workshop, or small group setting, Stonecroft women find ways to share the love of Christ.

- ***Stonecroft Military***—a specialized effort to honor women connected to the U.S. military and share with them the Gospel while showing them the love of Christ.

- ***Small Group Studies for Christians***—these resources reveal God's heart for those who do not yet know Him. The Aware Series includes *Aware, Belong,* and *Call.*

- ***Stonecroft Life Publications***—clearly explain the Gospel through stories of people whose lives have been transformed by Jesus Christ.

- ***Stonecroft.org***—offers fresh content daily to equip and encourage you.

Dedicated and enthusiastic Stonecroft staff serve you via Divisional Field Directors stationed across the United States, and a Home Office team who support tens of thousands of dedicated volunteers worldwide.

Your life matters. Join us today to impact your communities with the Gospel of Jesus Christ. Become involved with Stonecroft.

STONECROFT

Get started: connections@stonecroft.org 800.525.8627	Support Stonecroft: stonecroft.org/donate	Order resources: stonecroft.org/store 888.819.5218

Books for Further Study

Moore, Beth. *James: Mercy Triumphs.* Nashville, TN: Lifeway, 2011.

Morgan, Elisa. *Naked Fruit: Getting Honest About the Fruit of the Spirit.* Grand Rapids, MI: Revell, Baker Publishing, 2006.

Nystrom, David P. *The NIV Application Commentary.* Grand Rapids, MI: Zondervan Publishing House, 1997.

Pfeiffer, Charles F., and Everett F. Harrison, editors. *The Wycliffe Bible Commentary.* Nashville, TN: The Southwestern Company, 1962.

Whitney, Donald. *Spiritual Disciplines for the Christian Life.* Colorado Springs, CO: NavPress, 1997.

Stonecroft Resources

Stonecroft Bible Studies make the Word of God accessible to everyone. These studies allow small groups to discover the adventure of a personal relationship with God and introduce others to God's unlimited love, grace, forgiveness, and power. To learn more, visit **stonecroft.org/biblestudies**.

Who Is Jesus? (6 chapters)
He was a rebel against the status quo. The religious community viewed Him as a threat. The helpless and outcast considered Him a friend. Explore the life and teachings of Jesus—this rebel with a cause who challenges us today to a life of radical faith.

What Is God Like? (6 chapters)
What is God like? Is He just a higher power? Has He created us and left us on our own? Where is He when things don't make sense? Discover what the Bible tells us about God and how we can know Him in a life-transforming way.

Who Is the Holy Spirit? (6 chapters)
Are you living up to the full life that God wants for you? Learn about the Holy Spirit, our Helper and power source for everyday living, who works in perfect harmony with God the Father and Jesus the Son.

Connecting with God (8 chapters)
Prayer is our heart-to-heart communication with our heavenly Father. This study examines the purpose, power, and elements of prayer, sharing biblical principles for effective prayer.

Today I Pray
When we bow before God on behalf of someone who doesn't yet know of His saving work, of His great love in sending His Son, Jesus, of His mercy and goodness, we enter into a work that has

eternal impact. Stonecroft designed *Today I Pray* as a 30-day intercessory prayer commitment that you may use to focus your prayers on behalf of a specific person, or to pray for many—because your prayers are powerful and important!

Prayer Worth Repeating (15 devotions)
There is no place where your prayers to the one and only God cannot penetrate, no circumstance prayers cannot impact. As the mother of adult children, your greatest influence into their lives is through prayer. *Prayer Worth Repeating* is a devotional prayer guide designed to focus your prayers and encourage you to trust God more deeply as He works in the lives of your adult children.

Pray & Play Devotional (12 devotions)
It's playgroup with a purpose! Plus Mom tips. For details on starting a Pray & Play group, visit **stonecroft.org/prayandplay** or call **800.525.8627.**

Prayer Journal
A practical resource to strengthen your prayer life, this booklet includes an introductory section about the importance of prayer, the basic elements of prayer, and a clear Gospel presentation, as well as 40 pages of journaling your prayer requests and God's answers.

Prayer—Talking with God
This booklet provides insight and biblical principles to help you establish a stronger, more effective prayer life.

Aware (5 lessons)
Making Jesus known every day starts when we are *Aware* of those around us. This dynamic Stonecroft Small Group Bible Study about "Always Watching and Responding with Encouragement" equips and engages people in the initial steps to the joys of evangelism.

Belong (6 lessons)
For many in today's culture, the desire to belong is often part of their journey to believe. *Belong* explores how we can follow in Jesus' footsteps—and walk with others on their journey to belong.

Call (7 lessons)
Every day we meet people without Christ. That is God's intention.

He wants His people to initiate and build friendships. He wants us together. *Call* helps us take a closer look at how God makes Himself known through our relationships with those around us.

Discover together God's clear calling for you and those near to you.

These and many more Stonecroft resources are available to you. Order today to impact your communities with the Gospel of Jesus Christ. Simply visit **stonecroft.org/store** to get started.

If you have been encouraged and brought closer to God by this study, please consider giving a gift to Stonecroft so that others can experience life change as well. You can find information about giving online at **stonecroft.org**. (Click on the "Donate" tab.)

If you'd like to give via telephone, please contact us at **800.525.8627.** Or you can mail your gift to

Stonecroft
PO Box 9609
Kansas City, MO 64134-0609

Stonecroft

PO Box 9609, Kansas City, MO 64134-0609
Telephone: 816.763.7800 | 800.525.8627
E-mail: connections@stonecroft.org | stonecroft.org